ANIMALS

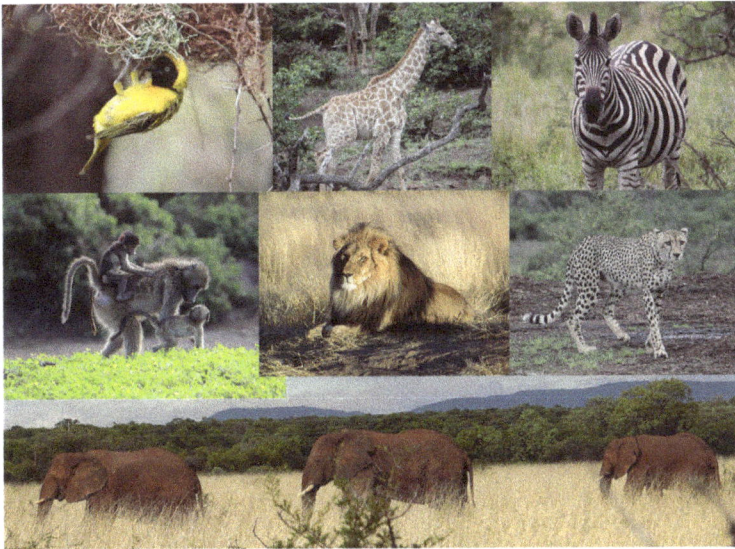

By Nadine & Pascale Eenkema van Dijk
Illustrated by Nadine, Pascale, & Reinier
Eenkema van Dijk

Library For All Ltd.

LIBRARY FOR ALL
DIGITAL EDUCATION FOR THE WORLD

Library For All is an Australian not for profit organisation with a mission to make knowledge accessible to all via an innovative digital library solution. Visit us at libraryforall.org

Animals

This edition published 2022

Published by Library For All Ltd
Email: info@libraryforall.org
URL: libraryforall.org

Library For All gratefully acknowledges the contributions of all who made previous editions of this book possible.

This book was made possible by the generous support of Save The Children.

Save the Children

Photos by Nadine, Pascale, & Reinier Eenkema van Dijk

Animals
Nadine & Pascale Eenkema van Dijk
ISBN: 978-1-922827-48-7
SKU02665

ANIMALS

The zebra has black and white stripes.

The big zebra is walking with her baby.

4

The giraffe has a
long neck.

She is eating leaves
from a tree.

The leopard has brown
and black spots.

The leopard is jumping.

The bird is small and
has beautiful colours.

She is building her nest.

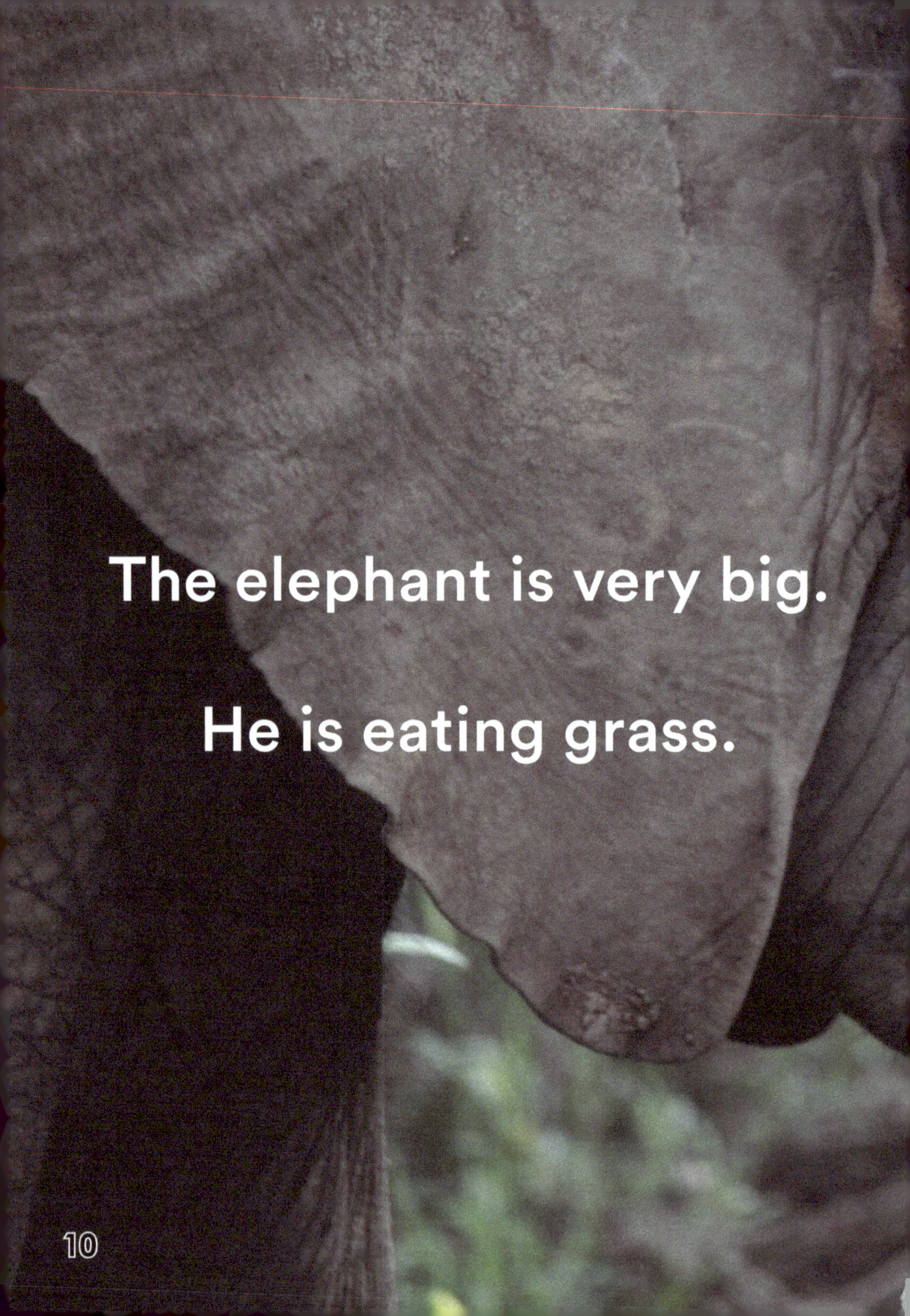

The elephant is very big.

He is eating grass.

The dad and mum
monkey love their baby.

The cheetah is
lying down.

The baby boars are
running behind
their daddy.

The hippo has a
big mouth.

He is yawning.

The antelope is walking with his friend.

The lioness walks through the wilderness looking for something to eat.

The hyena goes out at night to search for food.

She sleeps during the day.

The ostrich is a big bird.

She cannot fly, but she runs very fast.

You can use these questions to talk about this book with your family, friends and teachers.

What did you learn from this book?

Describe this book in one word.
Funny? Scary? Colourful? Interesting?

How did this book make you feel when you finished reading it?

What was your favourite part of this book?

download our reader app
getlibraryforall.org

About the contributors

Library For All works with authors and illustrators from around the world to develop diverse, relevant, high quality stories for young readers. Visit libraryforall.org for the latest news on writers' workshop events, submission guidelines and other creative opportunities.

Did you enjoy this book?

We have hundreds more expertly curated original stories to choose from.

We work in partnership with authors, educators, cultural advisors, governments and NGOs to bring the joy of reading to children everywhere.

Did you know?

We create global impact in these fields by embracing the United Nations Sustainable Development Goals.

libraryforall.org